Paris Pocket Guide 2023

**The Comprehensive,
Up-to-Date, and Essential
Guide to Paris' Top
Attractions, Restaurants, and
Hotels for First-Time Visitors**

Christopher L. Gerlach

Table of Contents

Introduction

Have you ever dreamed of visiting Paris? The City of Lights is a magical place, full of history, culture, and romance. But with so much to see and do, it can be hard to know where to start.

That's where I come in. I've been living in Paris for over 10 years, and I've seen it all. I've been to the top of the Eiffel Tower, I've seen the Mona Lisa at the Louvre, and I've even eaten at a Michelin-starred restaurant.

I've also been to the hidden gems of Paris, the places that most tourists never see. I've wandered through the Montmartre cemetery, I've had a picnic in the Luxembourg Gardens, and I've even been to a secret speakeasy.

In this book, I'm going to share all of my knowledge of Paris with you. I'm going to tell you about the best attractions, the best restaurants, and the best places to stay. I'm also going to give you tips on how to get around the city, how to save money, and how to avoid the tourist traps.

So whether you're a first-time visitor or a seasoned traveler, I hope you'll find this book helpful. With a little planning, you can have an unforgettable trip to Paris.

I still remember the first time I saw the Eiffel Tower. I was 12 years old, and I was on a school trip to Paris. We were walking along the Seine River, and the Eiffel Tower came into view. I was so excited that I started to cry.

I had always dreamed of seeing the Eiffel Tower, and now it was finally here. It was even more beautiful than I had imagined. The tower was so tall, and it sparkled in the sunlight. I couldn't believe that I was actually standing in front of it.

We spent the next few hours exploring the Eiffel Tower. We went up to the top, and we had amazing views of the city. We also learned about the history of the tower, and we saw some of the exhibits that were on display.

I had such a wonderful time at the Eiffel Tower. It was one of the highlights of my trip to Paris. I will never forget the feeling of seeing it for the first time.

Paris is a city that has something to offer everyone. Whether you're interested in art, history, food, or fashion, you'll find something to love in Paris.

If you're an art lover, you'll be in heaven in Paris. The city is home to some of the most famous museums in the world, including the Louvre, the Musée d'Orsay, and the Centre Pompidou. You could easily spend weeks exploring the art museums in Paris.

If you're interested in history, you'll also find plenty to see in Paris. The city is home to many historical landmarks, including the Eiffel Tower, the Notre Dame Cathedral, and the Palace of Versailles. You can easily spend a day or two exploring the historical sites in Paris.

And if you're a foodie, you'll be in heaven in Paris. The city is home to some of the best restaurants in the world, serving everything from traditional French cuisine to international fare. You could easily spend a week eating your way through Paris.

But Paris is more than just art, history, and food. It's also a city of romance. The city is full of beautiful parks, gardens, and bridges. It's the perfect place to take a stroll with your loved one.

If you're looking for a romantic getaway, Paris is the perfect destination. You'll find everything you need in Paris to create a magical and unforgettable experience.

Why Visit Paris?

Paris - A city that's synonymous with elegance and style - has many reasons why it should be on your list of travel destinations:

To begin with, its artistic heritage cannot be matched anywhere else in the world. With famous museums such as Louvre or Musee d'Orsay renowned globally for their collections as well as newer attractions like Centre Pompidou; it's clear why one could spend weeks exploring just art alone! The history buff will also have plenty here - from iconic landmarks like the Eiffel Tower or Notre Dame Cathedral representing proud symbols of Frances's past struggles against all odds down through time itself; there truly isn't anything missing from what once was Romes's northernmost outpost. Furthermore (and crucially) foodies won't be disappointed either; thanks to incredible restaurants and cafes serving everything from classic French cuisine to contemporary global fare. Spending a week dining here is easy - though watching your waistline may not be!

Lastly, for those seeking romance, there's no better city in the world than Paris. With its numerous parks and gardens providing stunning backdrops against which couples can make everlasting memories; from the Pont des Arts bridge which is famous for its love locks to every cafe which serves as a romantic hotspot - it is no wonder this city is known as the 'City of Love.' It is no secret that Paris is known as the global capital of fashion - with countless iconic designers calling this city home and unparalleled shopping opportunities available throughout its many neighbourhoods. But don't be fooled into thinking that all this vibrant destination has to go for it! Visitors are drawn in by endless attractions such as stunning artwork displayed in historic institutions like The Louvre; mouth-watering French cuisine found at bistros lining charming cobbled streets; not to be missed cultural events and festivals; and the city's legendary romantic ambience. Truly Paris has something to offer every kind of traveller.

What to Expect in Paris

What to anticipate in Paris is as follows:

The Eiffel Tower is one of the most recognizable structures in the entire globe. Any tourist to Paris must see it.

The Louvre is one of the biggest and most well-known museums in the world. The Mona Lisa and Venus de Milo, two of the most well-known pieces of art, are located there.

The Notre Dame Cathedral is a stunning Gothic structure that was constructed in the 12th century. One of the most visited tourist destinations in Paris is this one.

The Palace of Versailles is a former royal residence that is currently a museum. One of the most well-liked day trips from the city is to this place, which is nearby Paris.

The Sorbonne University is located in the Latin Quarter, an important historical area of Paris. It's a nice area to stroll about and take it all in.

Paris's fashionable Marais District is home to a wide variety of shops, eateries, and bars. It's a nice spot to buy and observe people.

The Champs-Élysées: The Champs-Élysées is a well-known Parisian road that is surrounded by stores, eateries, and cafés. The area is wonderful for strolling and window shopping.

The Arc de Triomphe is a triumphal arch that was constructed in the 19th century. It is a well-known tourist destination and may be found near the end of the Champs-Élysées.

The Tuileries Gardens are a lovely garden near the Louvre Museum. They're fantastic places to unwind and get away from the noise and bustle of the city.

The Luxembourg Gardens: The Luxembourg Gardens are yet another lovely park in the Latin Quarter. They're ideal spots for strolls, book reading, and picnics.

The core of Paris is bisected by the Seine River, which is a wonderful way to explore the city. A boat trip of the river is an option, as is a stroll along its banks.

The Meals: A cuisine lover's dream, Paris. Both upscale and informal dining establishments may be found in abundance in the city. Everything is available, including both foreign and traditional French food.

The people of Paris are renowned for their elegance and sophistication. Don't be offended if they don't smile at you; they are renowned for being a little aloof.

The Language: French is the official language of France. If you don't speak French, it's beneficial to brush up before you travel.

"The Culture" The culture of Paris is very diverse. Explore the various theatres, art galleries, and museums that are available. The entire year is filled with a variety of cultural celebrations and activities.

Everybody may find something to like in the city of Paris. Paris is a city you won't soon forget because of its history, culture, cuisine, and people.

How to get to Paris

By Plane

Paris is served by two major international airports: Charles de Gaulle Airport (CDG) and Orly Airport (ORY). CDG is the larger of the two airports and is located about 25 kilometers northeast of the city center. ORY is located about 18 kilometers south of the city center.

There are several airlines that offer direct flights to Paris from major cities around the world. Some of the most popular airlines that fly to Paris include Air France, Delta, British Airways, and American Airlines.

Once you arrive at CDG or ORY, you can take a train, bus, or taxi to the city center. The train is the fastest and most convenient option. The RER B train line connects CDG to the city center in about 30 minutes. The RER C train line connects ORY to the city center in about 20 minutes.

By Train

Paris is also well-connected to other European cities by train. The Eurostar train connects Paris to London in about two hours. The Thalys train connects Paris to Brussels in about one hour and 20 minutes. The TGV train connects Paris to many other major cities in France, including Marseille, Lyon, and Nice.

Once you arrive at a train station in Paris, you can take a taxi, bus, or metro to your final destination. The metro is the fastest and most convenient option.

By Car

Paris is located about 400 kilometers from London, 500 kilometers from Brussels, and 800 kilometers from Rome. If you are driving to Paris, you will need to take the A1 motorway. The drive from

London to Paris takes about 6 hours. The drive from Brussels to Paris takes about 4 hours. The drive from Rome to Paris takes about 10 hours.

Once you arrive in Paris, you can park your car in one of the many parking garages located throughout the city. Parking can be expensive, so it is best to book your parking in advance.

By Bus

There are several bus companies that offer direct bus service to Paris from major cities around Europe. Some of the most popular bus companies that travel to Paris include Eurolines, Flixbus, and Ouibus.

The bus is the cheapest way to travel to Paris, but it is also the slowest. The journey from London to Paris takes about 12 hours. The journey from Brussels to Paris takes about 8 hours. The journey from Rome to Paris takes about 24 hours.

Once you arrive in Paris, you can take a taxi, bus, or metro to your final destination. The metro is the fastest and most convenient option.

No matter how you choose to travel to Paris, you are sure to have a memorable trip. The city is full of history, culture, and beauty, and there is something for everyone to enjoy.

Getting Around Paris

There are several methods to navigate Paris. Some of the more well-liked choices are as follows:

The Metro is the quickest and most effective method to get across Paris. There are more than 300 stations and 16 lines. You may buy tickets at any Metro stop.

The RER is a regional rail network that links Paris to the nearby suburbs. There are more than 200 stations and five lines. Tickets are available at every RER station.

The Bus: Although it is a slower choice, using the bus is a fantastic way to see the city. In Paris, there are more than 500 bus routes. At any bus stop, you may buy tickets.

The Taxi: Although they might be pricey, taxis are a practical choice. They can be phoned in advance or hailed on the street.

The Velib is: More than 20,000 bikes are available for rent through the Vélib bike-sharing program. It's a fantastic way to navigate the city and take in the sights.

The Walking A fantastic way to see a city and get some fitness is by walking. The city of Paris is highly walkable.

A Paris Pass can be worthwhile to get if you want to remain in Paris for an extended period. With the Paris Pass, you have free entrance to several of the city's greatest attractions as well as unrestricted use to the Metro, RER, bus, and Vélib'.

Following are some suggestions for traveling to Paris:

Buy a Paris Pass: If you want to spend some time in Paris, it could be worthwhile to get a Paris Pass.

With the Paris Pass, you have free entrance to several of the city's greatest attractions as well as unrestricted use to the Metro, RER, bus, and Vélib'.

Learn the following fundamental French words: It is beneficial to learn a few fundamental words before you travel if you don't speak French. Travelling and interacting with locals will be much simpler as a result.

Be attentive to your surroundings: Even though Paris is a safe city, it's a good idea to constantly be cautious of your surroundings. Avoid carrying a lot of cash on you and watch out for pickpockets.

Enjoy your journey! The city of Paris is lovely and has a lot to offer. Enjoy yourself, take your time, and explore!

Where to Stay in Paris

Paris offers a broad range of lodging choices, from inexpensive hostels to opulent five-star hotels. Depending on your spending limit and hobbies, here are some recommendations for places to stay in Paris:

Affordable: several hostels in Paris provide economical lodging if you're on a tight budget. The HI Paris Bastille, the Generator Hostel Paris, and the Mama Shelter Paris East are a few well-liked choices.

Middle: several hotels in Paris provide decent value for money if you're searching for something in the middle. The Hotel Eiffel Trocadéro, the Hotel de la Place du Louvre, and the Hotel des Arts Montmartre are a few well-liked choices.

Luxurious: Several five-star hotels in Paris provide the finest of the best if you're searching for an opulent stay. The Ritz Paris, Hotel Plaza Athénée, and Hôtel de Crillon are a few well-liked choices.

When selecting a hotel in Paris, keep the following factors in mind:

Location: Given that Paris is a fairly walkable city, choosing a hotel with a handy location is essential. The Marais, the Latin Quarter, and Saint-Germain-des-Prés are a few of the most well-liked places to stay in Paris.

Budget: Paris may be costly, so it's crucial to establish one before you begin making travel arrangements. This will enable you to focus your search and locate a hotel that meets your requirements.

When selecting a hotel, bear in mind the amenities that are essential to you. Wi-Fi, a swimming pool, and air conditioning are a few of the most well-liked features.

Style: Because Paris has so much personality, it's crucial to pick a hotel that matches your unique preferences. Classic, contemporary, and boutique designs are a few of the more popular ones.

You may get the ideal lodging in Paris regardless of your preferences or spending limit. Paris is a city you won't soon forget because of its quaint districts, top-notch attractions, and delectable cuisine.

When to Visit Paris

When the weather is nice and there are fewer visitors, the ideal times to visit Paris are in the spring (April to June) or fall (September to October). While the winter (December to February) can be chilly and wet, the summer (July and August) can be extremely hot and congested.

According to your interests, the following is a more thorough analysis of the ideal dates to visit Paris:

Art enthusiasts: For those who enjoy art, spring or fall are the best times to visit Paris because the weather is pleasant and there are fewer visitors. The majority of the city's museums and art galleries host their most well-liked shows during this time.

History enthusiasts: History lovers should travel to Paris in the spring or fall when the weather is pleasant and there are fewer visitors. Many of the city's historical landmarks are less busy at this time, and you may appreciate them without the summer heat or the winter cold.

Food lovers: For culinary lovers, spring or fall are the best times to visit Paris because the weather is milder and there are fewer people. You may avoid the crowds at this time because many of the city's restaurants are serving their best seasonal fare.

The Romantics: Romantic travellers should go to Paris in the spring or fall when the weather is warm and there are fewer visitors. You may take strolls down the Seine, have picnics in the Luxembourg Gardens, and have candlelit dinners at quaint restaurants during this time, when the city is at its most picturesque.

You'll enjoy a fantastic trip to Paris no matter when you decide to travel there. Paris, a city with a rich history, culture, and gastronomy, has something to offer to everyone.

Budgeting for Your Trip to Paris

Here is an example spending plan for a 7-day trip for two to Paris:

Accommodations cost €1,000, transportation costs €200, activities €300, food €500, and souvenirs €100, for a total of €2,100.

You may change this budget to suit your requirements and interests. For instance, if money is limited, consider staying in an Airbnb or hostel as opposed to a hotel. By eating at less costly restaurants and taking advantage of cost-free activities like walking tours and museum visits, you may also save money.

Here are some suggestions for planning your Paris travel budget:

Establishing a budget before you begin your trip's preparation will prevent you from going over budget. Paris offers a variety of options to cut costs, including participating in free events and receiving discounts.

Be open to changing your plans if you want to find cheaper prices on accommodations, activities, and flights.

Don't overpack. You'll spend less in baggage fees the less you need to carry.

Take advantage of free activities. Walking tours, museum visits, and people-watching are just a few of the numerous free activities available in Paris. Eat at less-priced restaurants. Paris has a wide variety of wonderful eateries that are reasonably priced.

Use the public transit system to navigate Paris and save money on cabs and Uber rides. Purchase a

Paris Pass. With the Paris Pass, you have free transit and unrestricted access to several of the city's greatest attractions.

These recommendations can help you travel to Paris on a budget while still having a great experience.

Top Attractions

The Eiffel Tower

One of the most recognizable buildings in the world is the Eiffel Tower. Having been constructed in 1889 for the World's Fair, it is today a well-liked tourist destination. Visitors may reach three floors of the 324-meter-tall tower. Views of the city are available from the first level, panorama views are available from the second level, and a bird's-eye view of Paris is available from the third level.

From 9:30 am until 11:45 pm every day, the Eiffel Tower is accessible. Either online or in person at the box office, tickets are available. Depending on what level you wish to visit, different tickets have different prices.

Following are some suggestions for seeing the Eiffel Tower:

Pre-purchase your tickets. You'll save time and money by doing this.

Be there early. It's advisable to come there early to avoid the lineups because the tower may get quite busy.

Put on some relaxed shoes. There will be a lot of walking involved.

Pack a camera. You'll want to take pictures of the breathtaking vistas from the tower's summit.

Prepare yourself for crowds. Because the Eiffel Tower is a well-liked tourist destination, expect crowds.

Any traveller to Paris must see the Eiffel Tower. It is a well-known landmark that provides breathtaking city views.

Here are some more details on the Eiffel Tower:

French engineer Gustave Eiffel created the Eiffel Tower.

For the World's Fair in 1889, the tower was constructed.

Ironwork is used to construct the structure.

324 meters is how high the tower is.

Visitors can reach the tower's three floors.

Views of the city may be seen from the first floor.

The second level provides a bird's-eye view.

A bird's-eye view of Paris is available from the third level.

From 9:30 am until 11:45 pm every day, the Eiffel Tower is accessible.

Either online or in person at the box office, tickets are available.

Depending on what level you wish to visit, different tickets have different prices.

A very packed tourist destination is the Eiffel Tower. To prevent lineups, it is important to arrive early. The tower is a well-liked location for romantic gestures like marriage proposals. Visit the Eiffel Tower at night if you want a one-of-a-kind and unforgettable experience. The tower provides breathtaking views of the city while being colourfully illuminated.

The following information regarding the Eiffel Tower is fascinating:

With approximately 6.91 million people in 2015, the Eiffel Tower was the most-visited paid monument in the whole world.

After the Millau Viaduct, the Eiffel Tower is the second-highest building in France and the tallest building in all of Paris.

The Eiffel Tower was initially supposed to be demolished after 20 years, but it was kept around thanks to public demand.

Since 1913, the Eiffel Tower has served as a radio transmitter.

The James Bond movie "A View to a Kill" and the Disney movie "Ratatouille" are just two examples of the many movies and television shows that have included the Eiffel Tower.

Any tourist will undoubtedly have a lasting image of France after seeing the Eiffel Tower, an iconic monument. A visit to Paris must include a stop here.

The Louvre Museum

One of the most well-known museums in the world is the Louvre. It is situated in Paris, France, and it has a sizable collection of artwork from other countries. Since its founding in 1793, the museum has been accessible to the general public.

Some of the most well-known pieces of art in the whole world, such as the Mona Lisa, Venus de Milo, and Winged Victory of Samothrace, may be found in the Louvre Museum. A sizable collection of Egyptian antiquities, Greek and Roman sculptures, and Renaissance and Baroque paintings are also housed at the museum.

As a well-liked tourist attraction, the Louvre Museum may get quite busy. To escape the crowds, it is better to visit the museum early in the morning or late in the evening. Additionally, the museum is open until late on Friday and Saturday.

Any anyone visiting Paris should visit the Louvre Museum. With a wide range of artwork to view, it is a sizable and attractive museum. The museum is a fantastic resource for education on the development of art and culture.

Here are some more details on the Louvre Museum:

The largest art museum in the world is the Louvre.

Over 35,000 pieces of art are on show in the museum.

Except for Tuesday, the museum is open every day.

From 9:00 am to 6:00 pm, the museum is open.

On Tuesdays, the museum is closed.

Children under 18 are free to visit the museum.

On Friday and Saturday evenings from 9:00 pm to 11:00 pm, the museum is open late.

A well-liked tourist destination, the Louvre Museum may get quite busy. To escape the crowds, it is better to visit the museum early in the morning or late in the evening. Additionally, the museum is open until late on Friday and Saturday.

The Louvre Museum is fascinating for the following reasons:

Initially, the Louvre Museum served as a royal residence.

Amid the French Revolution, in 1793, the museum was established.

The Mona Lisa, a work by Leonardo da Vinci, is the most well-known artwork in the museum.

The Venus de Milo, a Greek figure of Aphrodite, is the most well-known piece of art in the museum.

The Winged Victory of Samothrace, a Greek statue of Nike, is the most famous item in the museum.

Any visitor will undoubtedly get a lasting image of the renowned Louvre Museum. A visit to Paris must include a stop here.

Here are some recommendations for visiting the Louvre:

Pre-purchase your tickets. You'll save time and money by doing this.

Be there early. It's wise to get there early to avoid lineups because the museum may get quite busy.

Put on some relaxed shoes. There will be a lot of walking involved.

Pack a camera. You'll want to take pictures of the wonderful artwork you see.

Prepare yourself for crowds. Because the Louvre Museum is a well-liked tourist destination, expect crowds.

Any anyone visiting Paris should visit the Louvre Museum. It is a renowned museum with a huge selection of artwork. The museum is a fantastic resource for education on the development of art and culture.

The Palace of Versailles

A historic royal palace called the Palace of Versailles is situated in Versailles, France, some 19 kilometres to the west of Paris. The Public Establishment of the Palace, Museum, and National Estate of Versailles has been in charge of managing the palace since 1995. It is owned by the French Republic and is overseen by the French Ministry of Culture. Versailles' palace, park, and gardens get around 15,000,000 visitors annually, making it one of the most well-liked tourist destinations on the planet.

King Louis XIII constructed the Palace of Versailles as a hunting lodge in the 17th century. The lodge was converted into an opulent palace by his son Louis XIV, who used it as the French capital and the hub of European power for more than a century.

Louis XIV and his successors substantially renovated and enlarged the palace, which reached its apex of opulence in the 18th century.

A huge collection of structures and grounds make up the Palace of Versailles. The Hall of Mirrors, the Grand Apartments, and the Royal Chapel are just a few of the more than 2,300 rooms that make up the palace itself. With a total area of approximately 800 hectares, the gardens are much larger. The gardens of the main palace, the gardens of the Petit Trianon, and the gardens of the Grand Trianon are the three principal divisions of the grounds.

One of the most well-liked tourist locations worldwide is the Palace of Versailles, which is a UNESCO World Heritage Site. Any traveller to Paris must see it.

Here are some more details on the Palace of Versailles:

Between 1661 and 1715, the Palace of Versailles was constructed.

Over 2,300 rooms make up the palace.

More than 800 hectares make up Versailles' gardens. A UNESCO World Heritage Site, the palace.

One of the most well-liked travel spots worldwide is the Palace.

Any visitor to the Palace of Versailles is going to be impressed by this wonderfully renowned site. A visit to Paris must include a stop here.

Following are some suggestions for touring the Palace of Versailles:

Pre-purchase your tickets. You'll save time and money by doing this.

Be there early. It's wise to get there early to avoid the lineups because the palace may get quite busy.

Put on some relaxed shoes. There will be a lot of walking involved.

Pack a camera. The breathtaking vistas of the castle and grounds are something you must document.

Prepare yourself for crowds. Be ready for crowds because the Palace of Versailles is a renowned tourist destination.

Any anyone visiting Paris must see the Palace of Versailles. It is a well-known monument with a fascinating past and beautiful grounds. The palace is a fantastic location to study French history and royal history.

The Notre Dame Cathedral

On the eastern side of the Île de la Cité in Paris, France, the Notre Dame church is a medieval Catholic church. The cathedral, one of the most well-known specimens of French Gothic architecture, is devoted to the Virgin Mary. The building process started in 1163 and was finished in 1345. The cathedral is renowned for its exquisite sculptures, huge rose windows, and flying buttresses.

Millions of tourists visit the Notre Dame Cathedral each year, which is a well-known tourist attraction. The Hunchback of Notre Dame, The Da Vinci Code, and The Tourist are just a few of the films and television series that have used the cathedral as a backdrop.

On April 15, 2019, a fire extensively damaged the Notre Dame Cathedral. Much of the cathedral's interior was destroyed by the fire, which also caused the roof and spire to fall. The cathedral's primary structure, however, was salvaged, and repair efforts are currently being made.

The Notre Dame Cathedral represents France and Paris. It serves as a reminder of the history and culture of the city. For many individuals, the cathedral serves as a place of devotion and a beacon of hope.

Here are some more details on the Notre Dame Cathedral:

A Gothic cathedral is the Notre Dame Cathedral.

The Virgin Mary is honoured at the church.

The cathedral was built starting in 1163, and it was finished in 1345.

The cathedral is renowned for its exquisite sculptures, huge rose windows, and flying buttresses.

Millions of tourists visit the Notre Dame Cathedral each year, which is a well-known tourist attraction.

The cathedral has appeared in several films and television programs and is a well-liked site for shooting.

On April 15, 2019, a fire extensively damaged the Notre Dame Cathedral.

A cathedral restoration project is now in progress.

Any tourist to Paris will undoubtedly have a positive impression of the Notre Dame Cathedral because it is such a stunning and well-known structure. A visit to Paris must include a stop here.

The following are some recommendations for visiting Notre Dame Cathedral:

Pre-purchase your tickets. You'll save time and money by doing this.

Be there early. It's better to get there early to avoid the lineups because the cathedral may get quite packed.

Put on some relaxed shoes. There will be a lot of walking involved.

Pack a camera. You'll want to document the magnificent cathedral vistas.

Prepare yourself for crowds. Be ready for crowds; the Notre Dame Cathedral is a well-liked tourist destination.

Any traveller to Paris must see the Notre Dame Cathedral. It is a well-known monument with a fascinating past and beautiful architecture. The cathedral is a fantastic location to study French and Catholic historical topics.

The Arc de Triomphe

One of Paris, France's most recognizable landmarks is the Arc de Triomphe. At the end of the Champs-Élysées, on the Place Charles de Gaulle, is where you may find it. In order to honour the military successes of Napoleon Bonaparte, the Arc de Triomphe was constructed. Although it was opened in 1806, it wasn't finished until 1836.

A huge triumphal arch, the Arc de Triomphe. It measures 50 meters in height, 45 meters in width, and 22 meters in depth. The stone arch is embellished with sculptures and reliefs. The "Marseillaise," a sculpture representing warriors heading to battle, is the most well-known piece atop the Arc de Triomphe.

A well-liked travel destination is the Arc de Triomphe. Every year, millions of people go there. Another well-liked location for protests and demonstrations is the Arch. When they invaded France in 1940, the German troops marched beneath the Arc de Triomphe. Students and employees congregated beneath the bridge in 1968 to demonstrate against the government.

A representation of France and its military past is the Arc de Triomphe. It serves as a reminder of the nation's triumphs and setbacks. The arch also represents fortitude and optimism. It serves as a reminder that France has overcome several obstacles and will do so in the future.

Here are some more details about the Arc de Triomphe:

50 meters high, 45 meters broad, and 22 meters deep describe the Arc de Triomphe.

The stone arch is embellished with sculptures and reliefs.

The "Marseillaise" is the most well-known sculpture on the Arc de Triomphe.

Each year, millions of tourists go to Paris to view the Arc de Triomphe, which is a well-known tourist attraction.

Another well-liked location for protests and demonstrations is the Arch.

A representation of France and its military past is the Arc de Triomphe.

The arch serves as a symbol of the nation's triumphs and setbacks.

The arch also represents fortitude and optimism.

Anyone who visits the Arc de Triomphe will undoubtedly have a positive impression of this stunning and well-known structure. A visit to Paris must include a stop here.

Following are some recommendations for visiting the Arc de Triomphe:

Pre-purchase your tickets. You'll save time and money by doing this.

Be there early. It's better to get there early to avoid the lineups because the arch may get quite busy.

Put on some relaxed shoes. There will be a lot of walking involved.

Pack a camera. The breathtaking views from the top of the arch should be documented.

Prepare yourself for crowds. Be ready for crowds because the Arc de Triomphe is a famous tourist destination.

Any traveller to Paris must see the Arc de Triomphe. It is a well-known monument with a fascinating past and beautiful architecture. The arch is a fantastic location to learn about French military history.

The Sacré-Coeur Basilica

On top of the Montmartre hill in Paris, France lies a Roman Catholic church called the Sacré-Coeur Basilica. The church, which was constructed between 1875 and 1919, is devoted to the Sacred Heart of Jesus.

Millions of tourists visit the Sacré-Coeur Basilica each year, making it a well-liked tourist destination. The chapel is a favourite hangout for creative types as well. One of the most well-known views in Paris may be seen from the top of the church.

A stunning and well-known monument, the Sacré-Coeur Basilica is certain to make an impact on every visitor. A visit to Paris must include a stop here.

Here are some more details regarding the Basilica of the Sacré-Coeur:

The white travertine stone that makes up the Sacré-Coeur Basilica.

The dome of the church is 55 meters in diameter and stands 83 meters high.

The church's interior is embellished with stained glass windows, mosaics, and sculptures.

Millions of tourists visit the Sacré-Coeur Basilica each year, making it a well-liked tourist destination.

The chapel is a favourite hangout for creative types as well.

One of the most well-known views in Paris may be seen from the top of the church.

The Sacré-Coeur Basilica serves as a testament to peace and optimism. It serves as a reminder that there is always hope for a brighter future, even amid sorrow.

Here are some pointers for visiting the Basilica of the Sacré-Coeur:

Pre-purchase your tickets. You'll save time and money by doing this.

Be there early. It's wise to get there early to avoid the lineups because the basilica may get quite busy.

Put on some relaxed shoes. There will be a lot of walking involved.

Pack a camera. You'll want to take pictures of the breathtaking vistas from the basilica's summit.

Prepare yourself for crowds. Be ready for crowds because the Sacré-Coeur Basilica is a famous tourist destination.

Any traveller to Paris must see the Sacré-Coeur Basilica. It is a well-known monument with a fascinating past and beautiful architecture. The

Basilica is a fantastic location to study French history and Catholicism.

The Musée d'Orsay

On the Left Bank of the Seine in Paris, France, there is a museum called the Musée d'Orsay. It is located in the old Gare d'Orsay, an 1898–1900 Beaux-Arts railroad station. The majority of the artwork at the museum was created in France between 1848 and 1914 and includes paintings, sculptures, furniture, and photographs. It has the biggest collection of Impressionist and post-Impressionist masterpieces in the world, including works by Gauguin, van Gogh, Seurat, Sisley, Degas, Renoir, Berthe Morisot, and Claude Monet. Before the museum's establishment in 1986, a large number of these pieces were shown at the Galerie Nationale du Jeu de Paume. One of the biggest art museums in Europe is this one.

Any art enthusiast visiting Paris must visit the Musée d'Orsay. Both the museum's collection and the structure itself are works of art. On the Left Bank of the Seine, and opposite the Tuileries Gardens, is where you'll find the museum. There is a sizable parking garage close by, and public transit is simple to use.

Tuesday through Sunday, 9:30 am to 6 pm, are museum hours. Mondays are a holiday. Adult admission is €16, student admission costs €12, and entry for those under 18 is €9. Seniors and organizations are eligible for discounts.

Given the size of the Musée d'Orsay, it may take many hours to view everything there. I suggest concentrating on the works by Impressionist and post-Impressionist artists if you don't have much time. The museum's higher levels are where you may find these pieces.

The following are some of the highlights of the museum's collection:

Claude Monet's "Water Lilies"
"Luncheon on the Grass" by Édouard Manet.
"The Dancers" by Edgar Degas.
"Bal au Moulin de la Galette" by Pierre-Auguste Renoir.

"The Card Players" by Paul Cézanne.

Vincent van Gogh's "The Starry Night" and Georges Seurat's "A Sunday Afternoon on the Island of La Grande Jatte"

The Musée d'Orsay's collection of artwork also includes sculptures, furniture, and photographs. Throughout the year, the museum also holds several transient exhibitions.

World-famous Musée d'Orsay provides a singular look into the art of the late 19th and early 20th centuries. I urge you to visit this fantastic museum if you're in Paris.

Listed below are some other suggestions for visiting the Musée d'Orsay:

To avoid the lengthy lineups, get your tickets in advance.

To avoid the throng, get there early.

Because you will be walking a lot, choose comfortable shoes.

Spend a good deal of time viewing the museum's collection.

Use the audio tour provided by the museum to learn more about the artwork.

Enjoy lunch with a view of the Seine River at the museum's cafeteria.

Purchase mementoes from the museum's gift store to remember your visit.

You may perhaps use this information to organize your trip to the Musée d'Orsay. You will have a great day exploring this incredible museum, I am sure.

The Centre Pompidou

Located in the 4th arrondissement of Paris, France's Beaubourg neighbourhood, the Centre Pompidou is a museum of modern art. It was created by the Richard Rogers, Su Rogers, Renzo Piano, and Gianfranco Franchini architectural team. The museum, which bears the name of the French president Georges Pompidou after whom it was commissioned, first opened its doors in 1977.

One of the most well-known tourist destinations in Paris is the Centre Pompidou. It has a sizable collection of modern and contemporary artwork, which includes murals, sculptures, photos, videos, and installations. A sizable library and research centre are also included at the museum.

The following are some of the highlights of the collection of the Centre Pompidou:

"Guernica" by Pablo Picasso.

Henri Matisse's "The Dance"

"Fountain," a work by Marcel Duchamp.

Salvador Dali's "The Persistence of Memory"

Campbell's Soup Cans by Andy Warhol.

The Centre Pompidou offers several temporary exhibits every year in addition to its permanent collection. The museum offers both adults and children a variety of educational activities.

Any art enthusiast visiting Paris should not miss a visit to the Centre Pompidou. Both the museum's collection and the structure itself are works of art. The museum is conveniently close to public transit and is situated in the centre of Paris.

Here are some more recommendations for going to the Centre Pompidou:

To avoid the lengthy lineups, get your tickets in advance.

To avoid the throng, get there early.

Because you will be walking a lot, choose comfortable shoes.

Spend a good deal of time viewing the museum's collection.

Use the audio tour provided by the museum to learn more about the artwork.

Enjoy lunch while seeing the city from the museum's restaurant.

Purchase mementoes from the museum's gift store to remember your visit.

You may use this information to organize your trip to the Centre Pompidou, I hope. You will have a great day exploring this incredible museum, I am sure.

Here are some more specifics on the Centre Pompidou:

Tuesday through Sunday, from 11 a.m. to 8 p.m., the museum is open. Mondays are a holiday.

Adult admission is €14, student admission costs €12, and entry for those under 18 is €9. Seniors and organizations are eligible for discounts.

The museum may be found in Paris, France at 75004 Place Georges Pompidou.

Rambuteau (line 11) and Châtelet (lines 1, 4, 7, 11, and 14) are the closest metro stations.

The museum offers a sizable bookstore and a restaurant with breathtaking city views.

The museum offers both adults and children a variety of educational activities.

The Latin Quarter

The Latin Quarter is a neighbourhood of Paris, France's 5th and 6th arrondissements. It is renowned for its vibrant atmosphere, bistros, and student population. Higher education institutions including the Sorbonne University and the Collège de France are located in the Latin Quarter. Additionally, it is the location of several historical sites and museums, including the Panthéon and the Jardin des Plantes.

It is simple to understand why the Latin Quarter is a popular tourist attraction. There is something for everyone to enjoy in this charming and unique neighbourhood. You will undoubtedly have a remarkable experience, regardless of whether you are interested in art, or history, or simply want to enjoy the lively atmosphere of the Latin Quarter.

The following are some of the prominent sights in the Latin Quarter:

One of the most prominent and historic institutions in the world is The Sorbonne University. Theologian and scholar Robert de Sorbon established it in 1257. Many well-known graduates of the institution call it home, including Victor Hugo, Simone de Beauvoir, and Michel Foucault.

The Panthéon: Constructed in the 18th century, the Panthéon is a mausoleum. Some of France's most well-known residents, including Voltaire, Rousseau, and Marie Curie, are buried there.

The Jardin des Plantes is a botanical garden that was established in the seventeenth century. It is among the world's largest and oldest botanical gardens.

Many different kinds of plants from across the world may be found in the garden.

The Cluny Museum was established as a museum in the nineteenth century. Its focus is on the history and art of the Middle Ages. The Lady with Unicorn tapestries is among the well-known pieces of art that can be found inside the museum.

Shakespeare & Company is a well-known bookstore that sells books in English. It was established in 1951. The bookshop is a well-liked hangout for writers and students.

The Latin Quarter is also home to a multitude of cafés, restaurants, and pubs in addition to these attractions. The area is a wonderful spot to unwind and take in the ambience of Paris.

The following advice is for travellers to the Latin Quarter:

The Latin Quarter is most enjoyable in the spring or fall. These times of year have moderate weather and fewer visitors.

The Latin Quarter is an area that is ideal for strolling. Several buses and metro lines may carry you around the neighbourhood if you get weary of walking.

A particularly secure area is the Latin Quarter. However, it is always a good idea to pay attention to your surroundings and take security measures to prevent small-time theft.

A fantastic area to people-watch is the Latin Quarter. The neighbourhood always has intriguing folks to view.

The Latin Quarter is a fantastic location to take in Paris's vibe. There is something for everyone to enjoy in this charming and unique neighbourhood.

The Marais District

The 3rd and 4th arrondissements of Paris, France, contain the historic Marais District. It is renowned for its winding lanes, quaint buildings, and lively atmosphere. It is clear why the Marais is a well-liked tourist attraction. There is something for everyone to enjoy in this charming and unique neighbourhood. You will undoubtedly have a remarkable experience, regardless of whether you are interested in art, or history, or simply want to enjoy the lively atmosphere of the Marais.

The following are a few of the top sights in the Marais:

Place des Vosges: Developed in the 17th century, Place des Vosges is a square. One of Paris' most picturesque squares is this one. There are many fountains in the square's centre, which is encircled by a colonnade.

Musée Carnavalet: Founded in the 19th century, the Musée Carnavalet is a museum. It is devoted to Parisian history. Several well-known pieces of art, including paintings, sculptures, and tapestries, may be found inside the museum.

The ancient palace known as the Hôtel de Sully was constructed in the 17th century. One of Paris' most exquisite residences is this one. The home is now a museum with a focus on French history.

The city hall of Paris is called the Hôtel de Ville. Built-in the 17th century, it is a stunning structure.

The Paris mayor and city council offices are located in this structure.

The largest Jewish quarter in Europe is located in the Marais. Numerous synagogues, kosher eateries, and Jewish enterprises may be found in the district.

Shops, dining establishments, and cafés line the street known as Rue des Francs-Bourgeois. It's fun to meander and people-watch on the street.

Place du Marché Sainte-Catherine: This plaza is the location of a market where fresh food, flowers, and other items are sold. The area is a wonderful location to people-watch and take in the energy of the Marais.

The Marais is also home to a multitude of cafes, restaurants, and bars in addition to these attractions. The area is a wonderful spot to unwind and take in the ambience of Paris.

The following advice is for travellers to the Marais:

The Marais is most enjoyable in the spring or October. These times of year have moderate weather and fewer visitors.

A great neighbourhood for walking is The Marais. Several buses and metro lines may carry you around the neighbourhood if you get weary of walking.

District safety is excellent in the Marais. However, it is always a good idea to pay attention to your surroundings and take security measures to prevent small-time theft.

An excellent area to people-watch is the Marais. The neighbourhood always has intriguing folks to view.

The Marais is a fantastic location to take in Paris' atmosphere. There is something for everyone to enjoy in this charming and unique neighbourhood.

Restaurants

The Best Restaurants in Paris for Fine Dining

There are numerous good dining options in Paris, a city renowned for its cuisine. Here are some of the top ones:

L'Arpège: In the 7th arrondissement of Paris, L'Arpège is a three-Michelin-star restaurant. Chef Alain Passard, who is renowned for using seasonal products, is in charge of the establishment. Even though the menu is always changing, you can always count on finding inventive and mouthwatering cuisine.

Le Bernardin: The 16th arrondissement of Paris is home to the three-Michelin-star restaurant Le Bernardin. The restaurant's seafood specialities, which come from all over the world, are well-known. Although the menu varies periodically, you can always count on finding fresh and tasty seafood. Guy Savoy: The 17th arrondissement of Paris is home to the three Michelin-star restaurant

Guy Savoy. The restaurant is well-known for its traditional French fare, which is cooked with great care. Although the menu is always changing, you can always count on finding sophisticated and mouthwatering cuisine.

Jol Robuchon: The 8th arrondissement of Paris is home to the three Michelin-star restaurants Jol Robuchon. The restaurant's contemporary French cuisine, which is made with the freshest ingredients, is well-known. L'Oustau de Baumanière: L'Oustau de Baumanière is a three-Michelin-starred restaurant that is situated in the town of Les Baux-de-Provence, approximately an hour from Paris. The menu varies regularly, but you can always count on finding inventive and delectable meals. The restaurant's Provençal cuisine, which is made with seasonal, fresh ingredients, is well-known. Although the menu varies depending on the season, you can always count on finding substantial and savoury food.

These are only a few of Paris's many great dining establishments. You're sure to locate the ideal place to have a memorable supper with all the alternatives available.

Here are some other recommendations for picking a good dining establishment in Paris:

Keep your budget in mind. It's crucial to establish a budget before you begin your search for fine dining establishments because they might be pricey.

Consider the cuisine you are interested in. You can find something you like at one of Paris' many exquisite dining establishments.

Reserve a space. Make a reservation in advance; fine eating establishments are sometimes busy. Dress accordingly. There is a dress code for fine dining establishments, therefore it's crucial to be properly attired.

Be ready to put in some time. It's common for fine dining lunches to be lengthy and unhurried, so plan on spending some time at the restaurant. Enjoy the journey! Enjoying a good meal at a fine restaurant is important.

The Best Restaurants in Paris for Casual Dining

Here are a handful of Paris's top casual eating establishments:

In the Pigalle neighbourhood of Paris, there is a casual restaurant called Bouillon Pigalle. The eatery is renowned for its superb and reasonably priced French food. Despite the menu's regular modifications, you can always count on finding traditional French fare like coq au vin, steak frites, and moules frites. Additionally, the restaurant offers a wide variety of wines by the glass.

Chez Denise is a relaxed bistro in Paris' 11th arrondissement. The eatery is renowned for its cosy ambience and traditional French fare. Although the menu fluctuates depending on the season, you can always count on finding rich and savoury meals like ratatouille, boeuf bourguignon, and duck confit. Additionally, the restaurant offers a wide variety of French wines.

A relaxed dining establishment called Le Fumoir can be found in Paris's 7th arrondissement. The restaurant's wood-fired barbecue and variety of grilled meats and seafood have made it popular. Even though the menu is always changing, you can always count on finding items that are savoury and fresh, such as grilled salmon, lamb chops, and octopus. Additionally, the restaurant offers a wide variety of wines by the glass.

A casual dining establishment called L'Épi d'Or is situated in Paris's 11th arrondissement. The eatery is renowned for both its inexpensive costs and excellent Jewish food. Despite the menu's regular modifications, you can always count on finding traditional Jewish fares like latkes, matzo ball soup, and cholent. Additionally, the restaurant offers a wide variety of Israeli wines.

In the Marais neighbourhood of Paris, there is a casual restaurant called Le Marais Gourmand. The eatery is renowned for both its extensive menu of French delicacies and its reasonable costs. Even though the menu is always changing, you can always count on finding a wide selection of traditional French meals like steak frites, moules frites, and coq au vin. Additionally, the restaurant offers a wide variety of French wines.

These are only a few of Paris's many informal eating establishments. With so many alternatives available, you're sure to locate the ideal restaurant where you can have a delectable dinner without going over budget.

Here are some other recommendations for picking a casual eating establishment in Paris:

Keep your budget in mind. You will undoubtedly discover something that fits your budget because casual eating establishments are sometimes less expensive than fine dining establishments. Consider the cooking style that interests you. There are many informal dining establishments in Paris, so you're likely to find something you like. Make a booking. It's crucial to make a reservation in advance, especially if you're going to a casual eating establishment during a busy period.

Don't overdress. You may dress casually because casual eating establishments offer a relaxed dress code.

Be ready to put in some time. Be prepared to spend some time at the restaurant because casual dining dinners are sometimes shorter and less leisurely than fine dining meals. Enjoy the journey! A terrific way to discover Parisian local food and culture is through casual eating. Enjoy the experience, of course.

The Best Restaurants in Paris for Budget Dining

Paris is renowned for its cuisine, but it can also be pricey. There are still many excellent places to dine on a budget, though. Here are a handful of Paris's top cheap eating establishments:

In the Latin Quarter, there is a relaxed bistro called Chez Marianne. The eatery is renowned for its superb and reasonably priced French food. Despite the menu's regular modifications, you can always count on finding traditional French fare like coq au vin, steak frites, and moules frites. Additionally, the restaurant offers a wide variety of wines by the glass.

In the 2nd arrondissement of Paris, there is a casual restaurant called Bouillon Chartier. The eatery is renowned for its substantial and reasonably priced French food. Even though the menu regularly varies, you can always count on finding traditional French fare like steak frites, moules frites, and pot-au-feu. Additionally, the restaurant offers a wide variety of wines by the glass.

An informal dining establishment called L'As du Fallafel can be found in Paris's 11th arrondissement. The eatery is renowned for serving some of Paris' greatest falafel sandwiches. The sandwiches are reasonably priced, excellent, and a wonderful opportunity to sample the regional food.

In the 10th arrondissement of Paris, there is a simple restaurant called Le Comptoir Libanais. The eatery is well-known for its tasty and reasonably priced Lebanese food. Despite the menu's regular modifications, you can always count on finding a wide selection of traditional Lebanese foods including hummus, baba ghanoush, and shawarma.

In the 10th arrondissement of Paris, there is a simple restaurant called Le Petit Cambodge. The restaurant is well-known for its tasty and reasonably priced Cambodian food. Even though the menu is always changing, you can always count on finding a wide selection of traditional Cambodian foods including amok, larb, and num banh chok.

These are just a few of Paris's many inexpensive dining establishments. With so many alternatives available, you're sure to locate the ideal restaurant where you can have a delectable dinner without going over budget.

Here are some other suggestions for selecting a Parisian restaurant with a reasonable menu:

Keep your budget in mind. You're guaranteed to discover something that fits your budget because budget eating establishments are frequently less expensive than fine dining establishments. Consider the cooking style that interests you. There are many affordable dining options in Paris, so you're likely to find something you like. Make a booking. It's vital to make a reservation in advance at budget eating establishments, especially if you're going to be there during a popular period. Don't overdress. You may dress casually because the dress code for budget eating establishments is informal.

Be ready to put in some time. Be prepared to spend some time at the restaurant because budget dining meals are frequently shorter and less leisurely than fine dining lunches. Enjoy the journey! A terrific way to enjoy Parisian culture and food on a budget is to dine out. Enjoy the experience, of course.

The Best Restaurants in Paris for Brunch

The following are some of Paris's top brunch restaurants:

Chez Denise is a relaxed bistro in Paris' 11th arrondissement. The eatery is renowned for its cosy ambience and traditional French fare. Although the brunch menu varies periodically, you can always count on finding robust and savoury items like ratatouille, boeuf bourguignon, and duck confit. Additionally, the restaurant offers a wide variety of French wines.

A relaxed dining establishment called Le Fumoir can be found in Paris's 7th arrondissement. The restaurant's wood-fired barbecue and variety of grilled meats and seafood have made it popular. Although the brunch menu constantly varies, you can always count on finding grilled salmon, lamb chops, and octopus as well as other fresh and savoury meals. Additionally, the restaurant offers a wide variety of wines by the glass.

A casual dining establishment called L'Épi d'Or is situated in Paris's 11th arrondissement. The eatery is renowned for both its inexpensive costs and excellent Jewish food. Even while the brunch menu regularly varies, you can always count on finding traditional Jewish fares like latkes, matzo ball soup, and cholent. Additionally, the restaurant offers a wide variety of Israeli wines.

In the Marais neighbourhood of Paris, there is a casual restaurant called Le Marais Gourmand. The eatery is renowned for both its extensive menu of French delicacies and its reasonable costs. Even though the brunch menu is always changing, you can always count on finding a wide selection of traditional French meals like steak frites, moules frites, and coq au vin. Additionally, the restaurant offers a wide variety of French wines.

In the Latin Quarter, there is a relaxed bistro called Chez Marianne. The eatery is renowned for its superb and reasonably priced French food. Even while the brunch menu regularly varies, you can always count on finding traditional French fare like steak frites, moules frites, and coq au vin. Additionally, the restaurant offers a wide variety of wines by the glass.

In the 2nd arrondissement of Paris, there is a casual restaurant called Bouillon Chartier. The eatery is renowned for its substantial and reasonably priced French food. Even while the brunch menu regularly varies, you can always count on finding traditional French fare like steak frites, moules frites, and pot-au-feu. Additionally, the restaurant offers a wide variety of wines by the glass.

An informal dining establishment called L'As du Fallafel can be found in Paris's 11th arrondissement. The eatery is renowned for serving some of Paris' greatest falafel sandwiches. The sandwiches are reasonably priced, excellent, and a wonderful opportunity to sample the regional food.

In the 10th arrondissement of Paris, there is a simple restaurant called Le Comptoir Libanais. The eatery is well-known for its tasty and reasonably priced Lebanese food. Even while the brunch menu is always changing, you can always count on finding a wide selection of traditional Lebanese delicacies including hummus, baba ghanoush, and shawarma.

In the 10th arrondissement of Paris, there is a simple restaurant called Le Petit Cambodge. The restaurant is well-known for its tasty and reasonably priced Cambodian food. Even though the brunch menu is always changing, you can always count on finding a wide selection of traditional Cambodian foods including amok, larb, and num banh chok.

These are just a few of Paris's numerous brunch establishments. With so many alternatives available, you're sure to locate the ideal restaurant where you can have a delectable dinner without going over budget.

Additional suggestions for selecting a brunch restaurant in Paris are provided below:

Keep your budget in mind. Setting a budget before beginning your search for brunch restaurants is crucial because these establishments may be pricey.

Consider the cuisine you are interested in. There are many brunch restaurants in Paris, so you're sure to discover one that suits your preferences.

Make a booking. It's vital to make a reservation in advance, especially if you're going to a brunch restaurant at a popular period. Don't overdress. You may dress casually because brunch places offer a relaxed dress code.

Be ready to put in some time. Be prepared to spend some time at the restaurant because brunch meals are often longer and less leisurely than fine dining dinners. Enjoy the journey! Experience the local cuisine and culture of Paris during brunch. Enjoy the experience, of course.

The Best Restaurants in Paris for Dessert

No dinner is complete without dessert, and Paris is renowned for its delectable cuisine. Here are a handful of the top places to have dessert in Paris:

A traditional French eatery called Carette may be found in Paris's first arrondissement. The eatery is renowned for its classy ambience and delectable sweets. Despite the seasonal variations in the dessert menu, you can always count on finding traditional French sweets like crème brûlée, tarte tatin, and profiteroles.

The bakery and chocolate Dalloyau are situated in Paris's 8th arrondissement. The store's delectable pastries and chocolates are well-known. Although the dessert menu is always changing, you can always count on finding a wide selection of traditional French sweets in addition to more contemporary dishes.

The patisserie Ladurée is situated in Paris' 16th arrondissement. The store's macarons are renowned as some of the best in Paris. The macarons are a delicious way to sample the regional cuisine and come in a range of flavours.

The 7th arrondissement of Paris is home to the Pierre Hermé patisserie. The establishment is famed for its inventive sweets, which Pierre Hermé, a well-known pastry chef, creates. Although the dessert menu fluctuates regularly, you can always count on finding something special and mouthwatering.

A chocolate shop named Jean-Paul Hévin is situated in Paris's 6th arrondissement. The store's delectable chocolates, which are created with the best ingredients, are well-known. The selection of traditional and contemporary chocolates is always available, even if the chocolate menu regularly changes.

These are just a few of Paris's many dessert-focused eateries. You're sure to locate the ideal eatery to enjoy a delectable sweet treat with so many selections available.

Additional suggestions for selecting a dessert restaurant in Paris include the following:

Keep your budget in mind. Setting a budget before beginning your search for dessert restaurants is essential because these establishments may be pricey.

Consider the dessert variety you're drawn to. You can discover something to suit your taste in one of Paris' many dessert restaurants.

Make a booking. It's vital to book a reservation in advance, especially if you're going to a dessert restaurant at a popular period. Don't overdress. You may dress casually because dessert places have an informal dress code.

Be ready to put in some time. Be prepared to spend some time at the restaurant because dessert dinners are often shorter and less leisurely than fine dining meals. Enjoy the journey! A wonderful sweet dessert is an ideal way to cap off dinner, and Paris is the ideal location to indulge.

The Best Restaurants in Paris for Coffee and Tea

Here are a handful of the top cafes and teahouses in Paris:

A traditional French café called Angelina may be found in Paris's first arrondissement. The café is renowned for serving some of Paris' greatest hot chocolate. On a chilly day, hot chocolate, which is created with fresh cream and chocolate, is a fantastic way to stay warm.

A traditional French café called Café de Flore is situated in Paris's 6th arrondissement. The café is renowned for its creative and literary ambience. Numerous well-known authors and artists have attended the cafe, including Ernest Hemingway, Simone de Beauvoir, and Jean-Paul Sartre.

A traditional French café called Les Deux Magots may be found in Paris's 6th arrondissement. The café is renowned for its creative and literary ambience. Numerous well-known authors and painters have attended the cafe, including Pablo Picasso, Albert Camus, and Simone Signoret.

A café called Rive Gauche is situated in Paris's 7th arrondissement. The cafe's view of the Eiffel Tower is well-known. The cafe is an excellent location to sip tea or coffee while admiring the cityscape.

A café called Le Fumoir is situated in Paris's 7th arrondissement. The cafe's wood-fired grill and variety of grilled meats and shellfish have made it popular. A wide variety of coffees and teas are also available at the cafe.

These are just a few of Paris's numerous coffee and tea establishments. You're sure to discover the ideal location to enjoy a delectable cup of coffee or tea with so many selections available.

Additional suggestions for selecting a coffee or tea store in Paris include the following:

Keep your budget in mind. Setting a budget before beginning your search is essential because coffee and tea establishments may be pricey.

Consider the sort of coffee or tea you would like to drink. You may find something to suit your taste in any of Paris' many coffee and tea businesses. Make a booking. It's vital to make a reservation in advance, especially if you're going to a coffee or tea shop during a busy period. Don't overdress. You may dress casually because coffee and tea places offer a relaxed dress code.

Be ready to put in some time. Be prepared to spend some time at the establishment because coffee and tea cafes are often a place to unwind and have a leisurely lunch. Enjoy the journey! A terrific way to unwind and take in the ambience of Paris is to drink coffee or tea. Enjoy the experience, of course.

Hotels

The Best Luxury Hotels in Paris

The Top Luxury Accommodations in Paris

Everyone may find something to enjoy in Paris, from its recognizable buildings to its famous art museums. Of course, a vacation to Paris would not be complete without staying in one of its opulent hotels.

Listed below is a selection of Paris' finest five-star hotels:

Hotels Plaza Athénée

On one of Paris's most upscale retail districts, Avenue Montaigne, is home to the five-star Hôtel Plaza Athénée. Having opened its doors for the first time in 1913, the hotel has a lengthy and storied history. Over the years, it has hosted several well-known visitors, including Grace Kelly, Coco Chanel, and Ernest Hemingway.

The Hôtel Plaza Athénée is renowned for its flawless service, opulent lodgings, and top-notch dining establishments. L'Obélisque and La Cour Jardin, two of the hotel's restaurants, have received Michelin stars. Additionally, it includes a rooftop terrace with spectacular city views, a spa, and a fitness facility.

The Hotel de Crillon

On the Place de la Concorde, one of Paris' most renowned squares, sits the Hôtel de Crillon, another five-star hotel. The hotel was constructed in the 18th century, and over the years, it has undergone several renovations. Numerous notable visitors have stayed there, including John F. Kennedy, Marie Antoinette, and Napoleon Bonaparte.

The Hôtel de Crillon is renowned for its tasteful furnishings, opulent lodgings, and first-rate service. The hotel's Epicure and Les Ambassadeurs restaurants both have a Michelin star. Additionally, it offers a spa, a gym, and a pool.

Le Bristol,

The Faubourg Saint-Honoré, another of Paris's most upscale retail areas, is home to the five-star hotel Le Bristol. The 1920s saw the construction of the hotel, which has since undergone several renovations. Elizabeth Taylor, Audrey Hepburn, and Charlie Chaplin are just a few of the notable people that have visited.

Le Bristol is renowned for its lavish furnishings, opulent lodgings, and first-rate service. Epicure and La Brasserie are two of the hotel's restaurants with Michelin stars. Additionally, it offers a spa, a gym, and a pool.

It's called "The Peninsula Paris"

A short distance from the Arc de Triomphe, on the Avenue Kléber, lies the five-star hotel The Peninsula Paris. The hotel was constructed in the 1970s, and throughout the years, it has undergone several renovations. Numerous well-known people have visited there, including Prince Charles, Michael Jackson, and Jackie Kennedy Onassis.

The Peninsula Paris is renowned for its tasteful furnishings, opulent lodgings, and first-rate service. L'Epicure, Le Chinois, and Le Fumoir are three of the hotel's restaurants that have received Michelin stars. Additionally, it offers a spa, a gym, and a pool.

Paris's Shangri-La Hotel

On the Avenue d'Iéna and with a view of the Eiffel Tower, there is a five-star hotel called the Shangri-La Hotel, Paris. The 1920s saw the construction of the hotel, which has since undergone several renovations. Numerous well-known people have visited here, including Audrey Hepburn, John Wayne, and Sophia Loren.

The Shangri-La Hotel, in Paris is renowned for its breathtaking Eiffel Tower views, opulent suites, and flawless service. L'Abeille, the hotel's only

Michelin-starred restaurant. Additionally, it offers a spa, a gym, and a pool.

These are just a few of Paris's numerous opulent hotels. Whatever your preferences or spending limit, you're sure to discover the ideal hotel to make your time in Paris unforgettable.

The Best Mid-Range Hotels in Paris

With good reason, Paris is one of the most well-liked tourist attractions in the world. The Eiffel Tower, the Louvre, and the Notre Dame Cathedral are just a few of the city's well-known attractions. It also boasts a thriving food and nightlife scene. However, visiting Paris may be pricey, particularly if you're staying at an upscale hotel.

There are still several excellent mid-range hotels in Paris if you're searching for a less expensive choice. These accommodations provide a convenient and comfortable stay without breaking the budget. The top mid-range hotels in Paris are listed below:

The Hotel de Fleurie

In the centre of the Marais neighbourhood sits the lovely hotel known as Hôtel de Fleurie. The hotel is built in a structure from the 17th century and offers opulent rooms and suites. A rooftop patio with breathtaking city views is also available at the hotel.

Elysées Ceramic

The chic hotel Elysées Ceramic is situated in Paris's 8th arrondissement. The hotel, which has contemporary rooms and suites, is located in a former ceramics factory. A rooftop patio with views of the Arc de Triomphe is also available at the hotel.

Hotel Abatial St. Germain

In the neighbourhood of Saint-Germain-des-Prés, there is a historic hotel called Hotel Abbatial St. Germain. The hotel has exquisite rooms and suites and is set in a 17th-century monastery. There is a Michelin-starred restaurant inside the hotel.

Avenue Hotel Tourisme

A contemporary hotel called Hôtel Tourisme Avenue may be found in Paris's 16th arrondissement. The hotel is located in a Victorian structure and offers upscale rooms and suites. A rooftop patio with views of the Eiffel Tower is also available at the hotel.

"Hotel Alhambra"

In the neighbourhood of Montmartre, there is a wonderful hotel called Hotel Alhambra. The hotel is located in a Victorian structure and offers opulent rooms and suites. A rooftop patio with views of the Sacré-Coeur Basilica is also available at the hotel.

The Castex Hotel

The Latin Quarter is home to the famous Castex Hotel. The hotel is built in a structure from the 17th century and offers opulent rooms and suites. There is a Michelin-starred restaurant inside the hotel.

Best Western Star Champs-Elysées

On the Champs-Élysées, there is a contemporary hotel called the Best Western Star Champs-Elysées. The hotel is located in a modern structure and offers chic rooms and suites. A rooftop patio with views of the Arc de Triomphe is also available at the hotel.

Inn at Palais de Chaillot

The Trocadéro neighbourhood is home to the famous Hôtel Palais de Chaillot. Elegant guest rooms and suites are available at the hotel, which is built in a 1937 structure. A rooftop patio with views of the Eiffel Tower is also available at the hotel.

Hotel des Commédies

The Opéra neighbourhood is home to the lovely hotel Hôtel des Comédies. The hotel is built in a structure from the 17th century and offers opulent rooms and suites. There is a Michelin-starred restaurant inside the hotel.

Hotel des Three Poussins

The Latin Quarter is home to the famous hotel Hôtel des 3 Poussins. The hotel is built in a structure from the 17th century and offers opulent rooms and suites. There is a Michelin-starred restaurant inside the hotel.

These are only a few of Paris's many excellent mid-range hotels. You're sure to discover the ideal hotel for your upcoming vacation to the City of Light with the variety of alternatives available.

Additional suggestions for picking a mid-range hotel in Paris include the following:

 Keep your budget in mind. The cost of a night in a midrange hotel in Paris can range from about €100 to €200. Consider your surroundings. Choose a hotel in the first, second, sixth, seventh, or eighth arrondissements if you want to be close to the city's top attractions. Think about the facilities you desire. Free Wi-Fi, air conditioning, and fitness facilities are amenities that some midrange hotels provide.

Examine reviews. Finding out what other guests have to say about a specific hotel through online reviews might be beneficial.

You can locate a fantastic mid-range hotel in Paris that will suit your demands and budget with a little forward effort.

The Best Budget Hotels in Paris

Don't worry if you're on a tight budget; Paris still has a ton of fantastic lodging options that won't break the bank.

Here are a couple of Paris's top cheap hotels:

Inn des Arts et Métiers

The Place de la République and the Notre Dame Cathedral are both within a short stroll of this lovely hotel, which is situated in the centre of the Marais neighbourhood. The motel has straightforward yet cosy accommodations, and the staff is welcoming and helpful.

Hotels du Centre

The Louvre Museum and the Palais Royal are both nearby this low-cost hotel's 2nd arrondissement location. The hotel has spotless, cosy accommodations, and the breakfast buffet is outstanding.

Hotels de la Paix

In the 7th arrondissement, close to the Musée d'Orsay and the Eiffel Tower, lies this tiny, family-run hotel. The hotel's staff is wonderfully nice and accommodating, and the rooms are basic yet attractive.

Hotel de la Place du Louvre

This hotel is the ideal spot for art enthusiasts to stay because it is situated just next to the Louvre Museum. The hotel has spotless, cosy accommodations, and the breakfast buffet is outstanding.

Hotels de la Sorbonne

The Sorbonne University and the Panthéon are both nearby this hotel's location in the Latin Quarter. The hotel's staff is wonderfully nice and accommodating, and the rooms are basic yet attractive.

These are just a few of Paris's many excellent cheap hotels. You can select the ideal accommodation for your upcoming vacation to the City of Lights with a little bit of study.

Here are some more suggestions for locating a cheap hotel in Paris:

Look for hotels that offer savings for booking online or for spending numerous nights, especially if you're going during the high season.

 Think about booking a less convenient hotel. Hotels outside of the city centre are frequently substantially less expensive. Look for hotels that include complimentary Wi-Fi or breakfast. Long-term, these can help you save a ton of money.

You may easily discover a fantastic hotel in Paris on a budget with a little forward effort.

The Best Hotels in Paris for Couples

The Best Couples Hotels in Paris

In one of the most romantic cities in the world, Paris, there is no shortage of accommodations for romantic getaways for couples. Everyone can find a place to stay in Paris, which offers everything from cosy bed & breakfasts to opulent castles.

A handful of the top hotels in Paris for couples are listed below:

In the centre of the city, close to the Champs-Élysées, lies the renowned Le Bristol Paris. The hotel has a long history of hosting kings and famous people, and your stay will be unforgettable thanks to its opulent suites and exceptional service.

Hôtel Plaza Athénée: This five-star establishment, which is situated on the illustrious Avenue Montaigne, is renowned for its opulent interior design, first-rate dining options, and breathtaking views of the Eiffel Tower.

Ritz Paris: This elegant hotel, which dates back to the 19th century and is situated on Place Vendôme, has long been a favourite of socialites and celebrities. The Ritz is renowned for its opulent lodgings, Michelin-starred dining establishment, and famed afternoon tea service.

Le Meurice: This five-star establishment is situated on the Rue de Rivoli and is renowned for its chic interior design, Michelin-starred dining establishment, and first-rate spa.

The Shangri-La Hotel in Paris is a five-star establishment that is situated in the city's centre close to the Arc de Triomphe. The Shangri-La provides magnificent city views, a top-notch spa, and a selection of restaurants.

Some lovely bed and breakfasts in Paris are ideal for couples if you're seeking a more private and cheap choice.

The top bed and breakfasts in Paris for couples are listed below:

Hôtel des Arts Montmartre: Situated in the centre of Montmartre, this quaint bed & breakfast has breathtaking views of the Sacré-Coeur Basilica. The hotel provides a welcoming ambience that is ideal for unwinding, and it has a pleasant atmosphere.

The Panthéon and the Sorbonne University are both within easy walking distance of the lovely Hôtel du Petit Moulin, which is situated in the centre of the Latin Quarter. The hotel provides a welcoming ambience that is ideal for unwinding, and it has a pleasant atmosphere.

The Louvre Museum and the Tuileries Gardens are both within easy walking distance of the lovely Hôtel de la Place du Louvre, which is situated in the centre of the Louvre neighbourhood. The hotel provides a welcoming ambience that is ideal for unwinding, and it has a pleasant atmosphere.

There is a hotel in Paris that is ideal for your upcoming romantic holiday, regardless of your spending limit or personal preferences. So begin making travel arrangements right away and share the romance of Paris with your special someone.

Here are a few more suggestions for organizing a romantic trip to Paris:

Choose a hotel that is centrally placed so you can easily tour the city. Reserve your hotel far in advance, especially if you are visiting during peak season. Make sure you reserve a hotel with a view so you can awaken to beautiful city views. Request information on the hotel's romantic specials, which frequently include items like champagne, roses, and in-room massages. Consider booking a few unique excursions during your visit, such as a picnic in the Luxembourg Gardens, a gondola ride along the Seine, or a candlelit supper at a Michelin-starred establishment.

You may easily organize a memorable romantic trip for your lover to Paris with a little preparation.

The Best Hotels in Paris for Families

There are many wonderful options available in Paris if you're seeking a hotel that welcomes families. Listed here are some of our favourites:

Bristol Le

One of Paris' most opulent hotels, Le Bristol is also one of the most welcoming to families. There is a special kids' club at the hotel with a range of activities to keep kids of all ages entertained. There is also a spa, a pool, and a rooftop patio with magnificent city views.

Hôtel de Crillon

Another famous hotel in Paris, the Hôtel de Crillon, is a fantastic option for families. A lovely garden, a playground, and a kids' club are all available at the hotel. A spa, a restaurant with a Michelin star, and a pool are also present.

Inlet Peninsula

On Paris's Right Bank stands the opulent hotel known as The Peninsula. The hotel has several family-friendly features, such as a kids' club, a pool, and a spa. A rooftop terrace with magnificent views of the Eiffel Tower is also available.

Meurice Le

On the Rue de Rivoli, there is a five-star hotel called Le Meurice. The hotel has several family-friendly features, such as a kids' club, a pool, and a spa. A Michelin-starred restaurant is also present.

Paris's Ritz

On the Place Vendôme, there is a historic hotel called The Ritz Paris. The hotel has several family-friendly features, such as a kids' club, a pool, and a spa. A Michelin-starred restaurant is also present.

These are only a few of the fantastic hotels in Paris that welcome families. You can choose the ideal hotel for your family's needs from the many options available.

Many of these hotels also have unique family packages that include breakfast, dinner, and kid-friendly activities in addition to the aforementioned facilities. These deals can help you save money while enhancing the quality of your trip to Paris.

Budget, hotel location, and amenities that matter to you should all be taken into account when selecting a hotel for your family. You can be sure to find the ideal hotel for your family's upcoming trip to Paris thanks to the wide range of excellent options available.

Here are some other suggestions for picking a hotel in Paris that welcomes families:

Think about where the hotel is. You should pick a hotel in a central location if you intend to do a lot of sightseeing.

Make sure the hotel has the features your family values. You should pick a hotel with a kids' club or playground if you have young children. If you have older kids, picking a hotel with a pool or fitness centre can be a good idea.

Read hotel reviews before making a reservation. You can get a decent picture of what other families thought of the hotel through this.

You can locate the ideal family-friendly hotel in Paris with a little preparation. Your family will undoubtedly love touring the city and taking advantage of everything it has to offer.

The Best Hotels in Paris for Business Travelers

A few considerations should be made before booking a hotel for a business trip. The first thing you should check is that the hotel is close to your meetings or other appointments and is in a convenient location. The amenities that are crucial to you, such a business centre, free Wi-Fi, and a fitness centre, should also be taken into account.

The top hotels in Paris for business travellers are listed below:

IHG Hotel InterContinental Paris - Champs-Elysées Etoile

Just a few steps away from the Arc de Triomphe, this opulent hotel can be found on the renowned Champs-Élysées. The hotel offers a range of services, including a business centre, fitness centre, and swimming pool, as well as roomy suites and rooms.

Paris, Le Bristol

On the Place Vendôme, in the centre of the city, is where you'll find this five-star hotel. The hotel has a Michelin-starred restaurant and is renowned for its outstanding service and exquisite decor.

Pullman Bercy Paris Centre

The Bastille Opera House is only a short stroll from this modern hotel, which is situated in the Bercy neighbourhood. In addition to chic guestrooms and suites, the hotel also features a business centre, a fitness facility, and a rooftop terrace.

Les Jardins de la Villa Hotel

The Saint-Germain-des-Prés district, renowned for its intellectual and creative ambience, is where this boutique hotel is situated. Along with inviting rooms and suites, the hotel also features a business centre, a fitness facility, and a garden.

The Hotel du Collector

This chic hotel is situated in the centre of the Marais neighbourhood, which is recognized for its ancient structures and cobblestone walkways. A business centre, exercise centre, and rooftop terrace are all features of the hotel's contemporary rooms and suites.

Paris's Shangri-La Hotel

On the Avenue d'Iéna, next to the Eiffel Tower, sits this opulent hotel. The hotel offers a range of services, including a business centre, fitness centre, and swimming pool, as well as roomy suites and rooms.

Meurice Le

On the Place Vendôme, a location renowned for its exquisite dining and luxury shopping sits this ancient hotel. In addition to a Michelin-starred restaurant, a business centre, and a fitness centre, the hotel offers beautiful rooms and suites.

Pullman Tour Eiffel in Paris

The Eiffel Tower is a short distance away from this modern hotel. In addition to chic guestrooms and suites, the hotel also features a business centre, a fitness facility, and a rooftop terrace.

Inn at the Paris Marriott Opera Ambassador

The Opera area, which is home to a big opera theatre and upscale stores, is where this four-star hotel is situated. The hotel provides cosy rooms and suites, in addition to a restaurant, business centre, and fitness facility.

Arc de Triomphe Sofitel Paris

Just a few meters from the Arc de Triomphe, on Avenue Kleber, lies this opulent hotel. The hotel offers a range of services, including a business centre, fitness centre, and swimming pool, as well as roomy suites and rooms.

Westminster Hotel

The Place de la Concorde, famous for its recognizable obelisk and fountains, is where this ancient hotel is situated. In addition to a Michelin-starred restaurant, a business centre, and a fitness centre, the hotel offers beautiful rooms and suites.

Paris's Radisson Blu Hotel Champs Elysees

Just a few steps away from the Arc de Triomphe on the Champs-Élysées is this modern hotel. In addition to chic guestrooms and suites, the hotel also features a business centre, a fitness facility, and a rooftop terrace.

Among the many excellent hotels in Paris for business visitors, these are just a handful. You'll find the ideal lodging for your upcoming business trip if you take your demands and budget into account while selecting a hotel.

Other Information

French Culture and Etiquette

France is a country with a rich and long history, and its culture is reflected in its people, its language, and its art. One of the most important aspects of French culture is its emphasis on etiquette. French people are known for their politeness and their attention to detail, and this is evident in the way they interact with each other and with visitors to their country.

Greetings

When greeting someone in France, it is important to use the appropriate form of address. For men, you should use "Monsieur" and for women, you should use "Madame". It is also customary to shake hands when greeting someone for the first time.

Politeness

Politeness is very important in French culture. It is always polite to say "bonjour" (hello) and "au revoir" (goodbye) when entering and leaving a place. It is also polite to say "s'il vous plait" (please) and "merci" (thank you).

Dining

Dining is a very important part of French culture. When dining in a restaurant, it is customary to order a main course and a dessert. It is also customary to order a bottle of wine to accompany your meal. When eating, it is important to use your utensils properly. You should never eat with your hands, and you should always use a fork and knife.

Clothing

Clothing is an important part of French culture. It is important to dress appropriately for the occasion. For example, if you are visiting a museum, you should dress in smart casual attire. If you are attending a formal event, you should dress in evening wear.

Tipping

Tipping is not customary in France. However, if you are happy with the service you have received, you may leave a small tip of around 5%.

Public Behavior

It is important to be aware of your surroundings when in public in France. It is not considered polite to talk loudly or to make a scene. It is also important to be respectful of other people's space.

Photography

It is important to ask permission before taking someone's photograph. It is also important to be respectful of private property.

French culture is rich and complex, and its etiquette is an important part of it. By following these guidelines, you can show respect for the French people and their culture.

Additional Information

Here are some additional tips for following French etiquette:

Always be on time for appointments.

Avoid smoking in public places.

Do not litter.

Be respectful of religious and cultural differences.

Learn a few basic French phrases.

By following these tips, you can make a positive impression on the French people and ensure that you have a pleasant experience in France.

French Holidays and Festivals

Paris is a city that celebrates life. There are always festivals and events happening, no matter what time of year it is. Here are some of the most popular holidays and festivals in Paris:

New Year's Day

New Year's Day is a public holiday in France. It is celebrated on January 1st. People typically celebrate by attending church services, eating special foods, and spending time with family and friends. In Paris, there is a large fireworks display over the Eiffel Tower.

Epiphany

Epiphany is a Christian holiday that celebrates the arrival of the Three Wise Men to Bethlehem. It is celebrated on January 6th. In France, Epiphany is traditionally celebrated by eating galette des rois, a cake with a hidden figurine inside. The person who finds the figurine in their slice of cake is crowned king or queen for the day.

Candlemas

Candlemas is a Christian holiday that celebrates the presentation of Jesus Christ in the Temple. It is celebrated on February 2nd. In France, Candlemas is traditionally celebrated by blessing candles and making wishes.

Mardi Gras

Mardi Gras is a Christian holiday that celebrates the last day of Carnival. It is celebrated on the day before Ash Wednesday. In France, Mardi Gras is traditionally celebrated by wearing masks and costumes, eating king cake, and attending parades.

Valentine's Day

Valentine's Day is a romantic holiday that celebrates love and affection. It is celebrated on February 14th.

In France, Valentine's Day is traditionally celebrated by exchanging flowers, chocolates, and other gifts.

Easter

Easter is a Christian holiday that celebrates the resurrection of Jesus Christ. It is celebrated on the first Sunday after the first full moon after the spring equinox. In France, Easter is traditionally celebrated by attending church services, eating special foods, and decorating eggs.

Ascension Day

Ascension Day is a Christian holiday that celebrates the ascension of Jesus Christ into heaven. It is celebrated 40 days after Easter Sunday. In France, Ascension Day is traditionally celebrated by attending church services and picnicking.

Pentecost

Pentecost is a Christian holiday that celebrates the descent of the Holy Spirit upon the apostles. It is celebrated 50 days after Easter Sunday. In France, Pentecost is traditionally celebrated by attending church services and eating special foods.

Mother's Day

Mother's Day is a holiday that celebrates mothers and motherhood. It is celebrated on the second Sunday in May. In France, Mother's Day is traditionally celebrated by giving flowers, cards, and other gifts to mothers.

Father's Day

Father's Day is a holiday that celebrates fathers and fatherhood. It is celebrated on the third Sunday in June. In France, Father's Day is traditionally celebrated by giving flowers, cards, and other gifts to fathers.

Bastille Day

Bastille Day is a French national holiday that celebrates the storming of the Bastille prison in

1789. It is celebrated on July 14th. In Paris, Bastille Day is traditionally celebrated by a military parade down the Champs-Élysées, fireworks displays, and public festivities.

Assumption Day

Assumption Day is a Christian holiday that celebrates the assumption of Mary, the mother of Jesus, into heaven. It is celebrated on August 15th. In France, Assumption Day is traditionally celebrated by attending church services and picnicking.

All Saints' Day

All Saints' Day is a Christian holiday that celebrates all saints and martyrs. It is celebrated on November 1st. In France, All Saints' Day is traditionally celebrated by attending church services and visiting the graves of loved ones.

All Souls' Day

All Souls' Day is a Christian holiday that prays for the souls of the dead. It is celebrated on November 2nd. In France, All Souls' Day is traditionally celebrated by attending church services and praying for the souls of the dead.

Christmas

Christmas is a Christian holiday that celebrates the birth of Jesus Christ. It is celebrated on December 25th. In France, Christmas is traditionally celebrated by attending church services, eating special foods, decorating Christmas trees, and exchanging gifts.

These are just a few of the many holidays and festivals that are celebrated in Paris. With so much to see and do, you're sure to have a memorable time no matter when you visit.

French Food and Wine

Paris is a city of food and wine. There are restaurants and cafes on every corner, and the city is home to some of the best chefs in the world. Whether you're looking for a casual meal or a fine dining experience, you're sure to find something to your taste in Paris.

French Cuisine

French cuisine is known for its rich flavors and its use of fresh ingredients. Some of the most popular French dishes include:

Crêpes: These thin pancakes can be filled with sweet or savory ingredients.

Croissants: These buttery pastries are a popular breakfast food.

Quiche: This savory tart is made with eggs, cream, and cheese.

Boeuf bourguignon: This beef stew is made with red wine, vegetables, and herbs.

Coq au vin: This chicken stew is made with red wine, bacon, and mushrooms.

Ratatouille: This vegetable stew is made with tomatoes, eggplant, zucchini, and peppers.

Soufflé: This light and airy dessert is made with eggs, sugar, and whipped cream.

Crème brûlée: This custard dessert is topped with a layer of caramelized sugar.

French Wine

France is home to some of the best wine in the world. The most famous French wine regions include:

Bordeaux: This region is known for its red wines, such as Cabernet Sauvignon and Merlot.

Burgundy: This region is known for its white wines, such as Chardonnay and Pinot Noir.

Champagne: This region is known for its sparkling wines.

Where to Eat and Drink in Paris

There are many great places to eat and drink in Paris. Here are a few of my favorites:

L'Arpège: This Michelin-starred restaurant is known for its modern French cuisine.

Le Bernardin: This Michelin-starred restaurant is known for its seafood dishes.

La Tour d'Argent: This historic restaurant is known for its duck dishes.

Café de Flore: This iconic café is a popular spot for people-watching.

Brasserie Lipp: This brasserie is a popular spot for lunch and dinner.

Angelina: This tearoom is known for its Mont Blanc dessert.

Ladurée: This patisserie is known for its macarons.

Pierre Hermé: This patisserie is known for its chocolates and pastries.

Paris is a city that celebrates food and wine. With so many great restaurants and cafes to choose from, you're sure to find something to your taste. And with so many different types of French wine to try, you're sure to find your new favorite. So what are you waiting for? Start planning your trip to Paris today!

French Shopping

Paris is a city of fashion, art, and culture. It is also a city of shopping. There are shops and boutiques on every corner, and the city is home to some of the most famous brands in the world. Whether you're looking for high-end designer clothes or unique souvenirs, you're sure to find something to your taste in Paris.

Where to Shop in Paris

There are many great places to shop in Paris. Here are a few of my favorites:

Champs-Élysées: This iconic avenue is home to some of the most famous luxury brands in the world, such as Louis Vuitton, Chanel, and Dior.

Rue Saint-Honoré: This street is known for its high-end fashion boutiques, such as Hermès, Gucci, and Prada.

Marais: This historic district is home to a mix of independent boutiques and vintage shops.

Saint-Germain-des-Prés: This trendy neighborhood is known for its art galleries, bookshops, and cafes.

Canal Saint-Martin: This canalside area is home to a variety of shops, including boutiques, restaurants, and bars.

What to Buy in Paris

There are many great things to buy in Paris. Here are a few of my favorites:

Fashion: Paris is a fashion capital, so you're sure to find the latest trends here.

Perfume: France is home to some of the best perfumeries in the world, such as Chanel, Dior, and Guerlain.

Food: Paris is a foodie's paradise, so you're sure to find something to your taste. From pastries and macarons to wine and cheese, there's something for everyone.

Art: Paris is home to world-renowned art museums, such as the Louvre and the Musée d'Orsay. You can also find a variety of art galleries and boutiques selling unique pieces.

Literature: Paris is a city of literature, so you're sure to find a great book to read. From classic French novels to contemporary literature, there's something for everyone.

Tips for Shopping in Paris

Here are a few tips for shopping in Paris:

Be prepared to spend money: Paris is an expensive city, so be prepared to spend money if you want to buy high-end fashion or luxury items.

Do your research: Before you go shopping, do some research to find out what stores and boutiques you want to visit. This will help you save time and avoid getting overwhelmed.

Bargaining: It is customary to bargain in some markets and boutiques in Paris. If you're not sure if bargaining is allowed, ask the shopkeeper.

Be aware of your surroundings: Paris is a safe city, but it's always a good idea to be aware of your surroundings when you're shopping. Don't carry too much cash or valuables with you, and be sure to keep an eye on your belongings.

Paris is a great city for shopping. With so many great stores and boutiques to choose from, you're sure to find something to your taste. So what are you waiting for? Start planning your shopping trip to Paris today!

French Transportation

Paris has an excellent public transportation system that makes it easy to get around the city. The most popular modes of transportation in Paris are the metro, bus, and RER train.

Metro

The metro is the fastest and most efficient way to get around Paris. There are 16 lines that crisscross the city, and most of the major tourist attractions are within walking distance of a metro station. Tickets for the metro can be purchased at any metro station or at tabacs (tobacco shops).

Bus

The bus is a slower option than the metro, but it can be useful for getting to places that are not served by the metro. Buses run throughout the city, and tickets can be purchased from the driver.

RER Train

The RER train is a regional train that connects Paris to the suburbs. There are five lines that serve the city, and tickets can be purchased at any RER station or at tabacs.

Taxi

Taxis are available throughout Paris, but they can be expensive. A taxi ride from the city center to the airport can cost upwards of €50.

Bicycle

Bicycles are a great way to get around Paris, especially in the summer. There are bike lanes throughout the city, and you can rent bicycles from a number of companies.

Walking

Walking is the best way to see Paris. The city is very walkable, and there are plenty of things to see and do within walking distance of most tourist attractions.

Paris has an excellent public transportation system that makes it easy to get around the city. With so many options to choose from, you're sure to find a way to get around that fits your needs and budget.

Here are some additional tips for getting around Paris:

Purchase a Paris Pass or Museum Pass. These passes give you unlimited access to public transportation and many of the city's top attractions.

Learn a few basic French phrases. This will help you get around and communicate with locals.

Be aware of your surroundings. Paris is a safe city, but it's always a good idea to be aware of your belongings and your surroundings.

Have fun! Paris is a beautiful city with something to offer everyone.

French Currency and Exchange Rates

The official currency of France is the euro (€). One euro is divided into 100 cents. Euros are issued by the European Central Bank (ECB) and are used by 19 countries in the European Union (EU).

Exchange Rates

The exchange rate between the euro and other currencies is constantly changing. You can find the current exchange rate online or at a bank.

Where to Exchange Currency

You can exchange currency at banks, currency exchange bureaus, and some hotels. Banks usually offer the best exchange rates, but they may have longer wait times. Currency exchange bureaus are typically faster, but they may charge a commission. Hotels often have currency exchange services, but their rates are usually not as good as banks or currency exchange bureaus.

Tips for Exchanging Currency

Here are a few tips for exchanging currency:

Do your research. Compare exchange rates before you exchange your currency.

Be aware of fees. Some banks and currency exchange bureaus charge commissions.

Ask about discounts. Some banks and currency exchange bureaus offer discounts for students, seniors, and members of the military.

Exchange your currency as soon as possible. The exchange rate is usually better when you exchange your currency before you travel.

Conclusion

Exchanging currency can be a hassle, but it's important to do it before you travel to France. By following these tips, you can get the best exchange rate and avoid paying unnecessary fees.

Here are some additional tips for using currency in France:

It is always a good idea to have some euros on hand, especially for small purchases.

Many businesses in Paris accept credit cards, but it is always a good idea to have some cash on hand in case a business does not accept credit cards.

Be aware of the exchange rate when you are making purchases. It is easy to overspend when you are not paying attention to the exchange rate.

If you are planning on doing a lot of shopping, it may be a good idea to get a credit card that does not charge foreign transaction fees.

Have fun! Paris is a beautiful city with something to offer everyone.

French Emergencies

Paris is a beautiful city with a rich history and culture. However, like any city, it is not immune to emergencies. If you find yourself in an emergency situation in Paris, it is important to know what to do.

Emergency Numbers

The most important thing to remember is to stay calm and call the appropriate emergency number. The three main emergency numbers in France are:

Police: 17
Fire: 18
Medical: 15

You can also call the European emergency number 112 from anywhere in France. This number will connect you to the appropriate emergency service.

Medical Emergencies

If you are experiencing a medical emergency, call 15. The SAMU (Service d'Aide Médicale d'Urgence) will send an ambulance to your location. If you are not sure if your situation is an emergency, it is always best to call and ask.

Fire Emergencies

If you see a fire, call 18. The pompiers (fire brigade) will come and put out the fire. If you are not sure if a situation is a fire, it is always best to call and ask.

Police Emergencies

If you see a crime in progress, call 17. The police will come and investigate. If you are not sure if a situation is a crime, it is always best to call and ask.

Other Emergencies

There are a number of other emergencies that may occur in Paris. If you are in an emergency situation that is not covered by the above numbers, you can call the following number:

General emergency: 112

What to Do After Calling an Emergency Number

Once you have called an emergency number, stay calm and wait for help to arrive. If you are able, try to provide as much information as possible to the emergency operator. This information will help them to send the appropriate help to your location.

Aftermath of an Emergency

After an emergency, it is important to take care of yourself. If you have been injured, seek medical attention. If you have been traumatized by the experience, talk to a friend, family member, or therapist.

Tips for Avoiding Emergencies

There are a number of things you can do to avoid emergencies. These include:

 Be aware of your surroundings.
 Stay in well-lit areas.
 Avoid walking alone at night.
 Trust your instincts. If you feel unsafe, leave the situation.

By knowing what to do in an emergency, you can help to ensure your safety and the safety of others. If you find yourself in an emergency situation in Paris, remember to stay calm and call the appropriate emergency number.

French Phrasebook

Basics

Hello: Bonjour (bohn-zhoor)
Goodbye: Au revoir (oh reh-vwahr)

Please: S'il vous plaît (seel voo play)

Thank you: Merci (mehr-see)

You're welcome: De rien (duh ree-ahn)

Excuse me: Pardon (pah-rohn)

I don't understand: Je ne comprends pas (zhuh nuh kohn-prohn pah)

Can you help me?: Pouvez-vous m'aider? (poo-vay voo may-day-ay)

Do you speak English?: Parlez-vous anglais? (par-lay voo ahng-lay)

I speak a little French: Je parle un peu français (zhuh parl uhn poo frawn-say)

I don't speak French: Je ne parle pas français (zhuh nuh parl pah frawn-say)

Greetings

Good morning: Bonjour (bohn-zhoor)

Good afternoon: Bon après-midi (bohn ah-preh-mee-dee)

Good evening: Bonsoir (bohn-swahr)

Good night: Bonne nuit (bohn nwee)

How are you?: Comment allez-vous? (koh-moh ah-lay voo)

I am fine: Je vais bien (zhuh vay bee-ehn)

And you?: Et vous? (ay voo)

Getting Around

Where is the bathroom?: Où sont les toilettes? (ooh sohn leh twah-LET)

I am lost: Je suis perdu (zhuh swee pehr-doo)

Can you help me find my way?: Pouvez-vous m'aider à trouver mon chemin? (poo-vay voo may-day-ay ah troo-vay moh shah-mehn)

I need to go to the train station: Je dois aller à la gare (zhuh doh ah-lay ah lah gar)

I need to go to the bus station: Je dois aller à la gare routière (zhuh doh ah-lay ah lah gar roo-teer)

I need to go to the airport: Je dois aller à l'aéroport (zhuh doh ah-lay ah lah-eh-roh-por)

How much does a ticket to Paris cost?: Combien coûte un billet pour Paris? (koh-bee-ahn koot uhn bee-yeh puhr pa-ree)

I would like a ticket to Paris, please: Je voudrais un billet pour Paris, s'il vous plaît (zhuh voodray uhn bee-yeh puhr pa-ree, seel voo play)

The train leaves at what time?: Le train part à quelle heure? (luh trahn par ah kel ur)

Where is the platform for the train to Paris?: Où est le quai pour le train pour Paris? (ooh sohn luh kay poor luh trahn poor pa-ree)

I have my ticket: J'ai mon billet (zhah may mohn bee-yeh)

Thank you for your help: Merci pour votre aide (mehr-see poor voo-truh ayd)

Accommodation

I would like a room, please: Je voudrais une chambre, s'il vous plaît (zhuh voodray uhn shahn-breh, seel voo play)

Do you have a room with a view?: Avez-vous une chambre avec vue? (ah-vay voo uhn shahn-breh ah-veh vwee)

How much is the room per night?: Combien coûte la chambre par nuit? (koh-bee-ahn koot lah shahn-breh par nwee)

I would like a room for one night: Je voudrais une chambre pour une nuit (zhuh voodray uhn shahn-breh poor ewn nwee)

I would like a room for two nights: Je voudrais une chambre pour deux nuits (zhuh voodray uhn shahn-breh poor duh nwee)

I would like a room with a double bed: Je voudrais une chambre avec un lit double (zhuh voodray uhn shahn

Visa Information

If you are planning a trip to Paris, you will need to obtain a visa from the French government. The type of visa you need will depend on the purpose of your visit. For example, if you are traveling to Paris for tourism, you will need a tourist visa. If you are traveling to Paris for business, you will need a business visa.

There are two main types of French visas: short-term visas and long-term visas. Short-term visas are valid for up to 90 days, while long-term visas are valid for more than 90 days.

Short-Term Visas

Short-term visas are for people who are traveling to France for tourism, business, or to visit family or friends. There are several different types of short-term visas, including:

Tourist visa: This visa is for people who are traveling to France for tourism. Tourist visas are valid for up to 90 days within a 180-day period.

Business visa: This visa is for people who are traveling to France for business. Business visas are valid for up to 90 days within a 180-day period.

Family visa: This visa is for people who are traveling to France to visit family or friends. Family visas are valid for up to 90 days within a 180-day period.

Long-Term Visas

Long-term visas are for people who are planning to stay in France for more than 90 days. There are several different types of long-term visas, including:

Student visa: This visa is for people who are planning to study in France. Student visas are valid for the duration of your studies.

Work visa: This visa is for people who are planning to work in France. Work visas are valid for the duration of your employment.

Residence visa: This visa is for people who are planning to live in France permanently. Residence visas are valid for up to five years.

How to Apply for a French Visa

To apply for a French visa, you will need to submit an application form to the French embassy or consulate in your home country. You will also need to provide the following documents:

Passport: Your passport must be valid for at least three months after the end of your planned stay in France.

Visa application form: You can download the visa application form from the French embassy or consulate website.

Passport-size photos: You will need two passport-size photos that meet the French government's requirements.

Proof of travel insurance: You will need to provide proof of travel insurance that covers you for the duration of your stay in France.

Proof of financial support: You will need to provide proof that you have enough money to cover your expenses during your stay in France.

Invitation letter (if applicable): If you are applying for a visa for a specific purpose, such as business or study, you may need to provide an invitation letter from the person or organization that is inviting you to France.

The application process for a French visa can take several weeks, so it is important to apply well in advance of your planned travel date.

Once you have submitted your application, you will be interviewed by a French consular officer. The consular officer will ask you questions about your trip to France and your reasons for visiting.

If your application is approved, you will be issued a visa. The visa will be stamped in your passport and will specify the purpose of your visit, the dates of your stay, and the number of entries allowed.

It is important to note that the French government reserves the right to deny a visa application for any reason.

For more information on French visas, please visit the French embassy or consulate website in your home country.

Printed in Great Britain
by Amazon

22945132R00076